Mythology vs. Modernity How Political, Social, and Ethical Ideologies impacted upon graphic design in the 20th century Case Studies of Germany and the Soviet Union

By Barry Vale

In memory of my Dad, Uncle and Sister

For my wife and children, Aunt, in laws, nieces and great niece

Special mention to Muz, a man wiser than he gives himself credit for

Contents

Abstract

The following work will discuss whether mythology or modernity
had the greatest impact upon the political, social, and ethical
ideologies that were closely linked to or had an influence upon
graphic design and artistic culture during the twentieth century. The
main focus of this dissertation will be to describe the often-complex
relationship between mythology and modernity in relation to
political, social, and ethical ideologies with particular reference to
Germany and, to a lesser extent the Soviet Union, essentially
between 1914 and the early 1930s. Germany and the Soviet Union
were chosen as the main case studies for this dissertation, due to
them being the countries that had the most complex situations, and
often they had a highly contradictory relationship between
mythology and modernity in the political, social, and ethical
ideologies that influenced graphic design. Germany is of particular
interest due to the clash between mythology and modernity at the
end of the imperial regime, throughout the short and turbulent
Weimar Republic and most strikingly during the Third Reich.

Imperial Germany had a government that was autocratic in nature,
the Weimar Republic allowed greater cultural diversity, yet suffered
from political and economic weaknesses that allowed Adolf Hitler to
bring the Third Reich into existence. In the Third Reich, it was
Hitler who determined what graphic design was acceptable and
pragmatic and which forms of it were politically, socially, as well as
ethically unacceptable (just as he did with everything else). As will
be mentioned Adolf Hitler's dislike of anything related to graphic
design or architecture if known widely enough could be as effective
at preventing things happening or closing down pre-existing
organisations as any decree or government legislation.

The Soviet Union also arguably interchanged mythology and
modernity in the political, social and ethical ideologies that
underpinned its graphic design, culture, and its architecture as well
as the governing regime. The Communist regime in the Soviet
Union and the Nazi regime in Germany had radical agendas that
were intended to transform the politics and the society of the

countries they ruled over. Both regimes had also intended to alter the political, social, and ethical ideologies of their populations through propaganda, indoctrination, and repression when required. For both regimes graphic design was just one of many ways to achieve their political, social, and ethical objectives, a method that they wished to control and even suppress if that suited their particular objectives and prejudices. These regimes could also find people that could use graphic design techniques to carry out their objectives whilst the formally qualified graphic designers were not used due to doubts over having suitable political, social, and ethical beliefs.

Introduction

Germany's defeat in the First World War and the collapse of the
Imperial regime had major political, social and ethical consequences
that were not just confined to the field of graphic design. Prior to the
First World War, the German government had built up the
mythology of the invincibility of the German army, strengthened by
the modernity and dynamic growth of its economy and its advanced
industrial complexes. Germany's rising economic production and
the ability to make industrial products effectively meant that
Germany's power was widely viewed as increasing, a cause for
national pride, and also a cause of international concerns that poised
a challenge to peace. German militaristic culture and its ambitions
to be a great power contributed to the outbreak of the First World
War, as did the decision to back all of Austria-Hungary's demands
against Serbia (Fulbrook, 1991, p.3). The Imperial German
government used propaganda to maintain the war effort in the wake
of heavy fatalities and severe shortages at home, due to the
effectiveness of the Royal Navy blockade. The failure of the
German spring offensives of 1918 brought about the final collapse
(Roberts, 1996, p.455).

Around the issue of German surrender in 1918 myths and counter
myths would abound. German nationalists claimed that Socialists,
Social Democrats, the Centre parties, and the Jews had betrayed the
country and its army. Such arguments were put forward by the
leading German generals, most notably Ludendorff to deflect from
their failures during the war. Other elements in Germany that
favoured modernity were those that supported the Weimar Republic
most strongly (although that support was not always returned by the
Weimar authorities). The ideological conflicts between left and right
would last until the Nazi Party came into power. Once the Nazis
gained power they intended to radically alter the political, social, and
ethical ideologies that dominated Germany through whatever means
they had to use. The social and ethical alterations would revolve
around cleansing the country of political, social, and racial
undesirables (Bullock, 1991, p.74).

The effectiveness of German propaganda during the First World War; the political, social, and ethical ideologies and their impact upon graphic design in Germany will discussed in chapters 1 to 3 as well as in the conclusions. The influence, innovations, and the subsequent legacy that the Bauhaus school had on graphic design in Germany and beyond will be scrutinised in greater detail.

In Germany the movement most closely linked to the concepts of modernity, rather than the concepts of mythology in graphic design would become known as the Bauhaus school after the graphic design school that opened at Weimar in 1919. The leading members of the future Bauhaus school were frequently working as architects and artists before the outbreak of the First World War in August 1914 (some of them in countries that fought against Germany). These artists and architects were equally committed to the concept of modernity and the political ideology of socialism. Ironically enough, the modernist concepts that would form the basis of the Bauhaus school were heavily influenced by British architecture, except for the Germans had in the vast majority of cases kept their allegiance to socialist ideals (Hobsbawm, 1987 p. 225).

From its inception the Bauhaus had a mission simple to drive forward its work, projects, and its teaching. That publicly stated aim was 'The Building of the Future'. The school hoped to make graphic design more accessible and pragmatic to help modernise the economy and help transform art and culture (www.bauhaus/archiv) Rohe argued that the modernist approach apparent within the Bauhaus which, was reflected in its graphic design and architecture would eventually become widely accepted. Modernist glass and steel structures although not popular with contemporaries would become symbolic of the Weimar era (Weimar Source Book, p. 439).

There was a competing stronger current in German culture that stressed the cultural, ethical and in more versions the racial superiority of the German nation above all other nations. This vision of a culturally superior Germany was favoured by most right wing groups throughout Imperial Germany, the Weimar Republic and was part of the extreme ideological basis of the Nazi party that came to power in 1933. For the German right wing nationalists' culture went further than occasional trips to the theatre or the cinema. Culture to them was part of the mythology of the greatness of the German people. Such strong and wide-ranging notions of nationalism go a long way towards explaining the highly militaristic nature of both Imperial Germany and the Third Reich. If anything, the militarism of the Third Reich was the most potent form as it was combined with the drive for racial purity, as well as plans to exterminate Communism and the Jews (Bullock, 1991 p. 76).

The emergence of the Communist regime in the Soviet Union also led to a mixture of mythology and modernity influencing the political, social, and ethical ideologies on graphic design. The Communist regime that took power in October 1917 to establish Marxism-Leninism across the former Russian Empire in what eventually became known as the Soviet Union. To secure its future the Communist regime used myths about the struggle to bring revolution, combined with the modernist urges, to end the political, social, industrial, and economic backwardness of the Soviet Union (Hobsbawm, 1994 p. 63). The Soviet regime maintained its grip on power through often large-scale brutal repression, the extensive use of official propaganda and censorship, and systems of party and government patronage. Under the cruel rule of Joseph Stalin the use of all these methods reached its systematic and violent peak with his campaigns to modernise the Soviet Union and crush all opposition real or made up (James, 2003 p. 61). The role of mythology and modernity in the graphic design of the Soviet Union will be discussed in chapter 4 and the conclusions.

Chapter 1 Mythology, Modernity, and the collapse of Imperial Germany

Imperial Germany had a rich culture, with mythological and militaristic ideologies seeming to dominate less popular modernist tendencies. The appeal of mythological ideology and heavily military influenced nationalism are linked with German history and the struggle to create a united Germany. Many Germans prided themselves upon their own culture. Imperial Germany for instance, had popular and successful theatres, which had expanded in actual numbers, as well as in the size of their audiences. Musically the pre-war period witnessed the peak in popularity of Richard Wagner's operas, laden as they were with mythology and heroic references. Imperial Germany saw the foundation of the precursor of the Bauhaus school in the form of the Werkbund as early as 1907 under the auspices of the renowned architect Hermann Muthesuis. Like the Bauhaus the Werkbund was intended to improve the efficiency of the industrial designs and machinery used by German businesses. The emphasis was upon modernity to drive forward economic growth. Modernity had also begun to influence art and graphic design (Watkins, 2005, p. 598). Glass and steel were the materials preferred by the Werkbund designers, a preference that continued with the Bauhaus. That continuation is not surprising as designers such as Gropius and Rohe worked within both groups. The styles that were later further developed by the Bauhaus were evident at the Cologne Werkbund Exhibition held shortly before the First World War (Weimar Source Book, p. 429).

At this point in history, Germany was becoming an increasingly powerful country, with a strong economy and a powerful army. Its government was undemocratic, and there was a strong sense of nationalism. Modernity was not rejected, just harnessed to increase the country's wealth and power (Burns, 1995 p.12). As will examined German designers had their design and political ideas radicalised by the First World War. However the ruined state of the German economy restricted new constructions before 1924 (Weimar Source Book, p. 429).

As a united country Imperial Germany owed its very existence to war, or three wars to be exact. Prussia and Austria had been rivals for the position of the leading German nation, Prussian policy aimed to achieve a united Germany but that seemed to be an unlikely dream. Under the Chancellorship of Count Otto von Bismarck the Prussians gained decisive victories over Denmark, Austria, and then France. A single German empire was forged with the Prussian King becoming the German Kaiser (Rayner & Stapley, 2006, p.92). In Imperial Germany, popular culture and mythology centred on the army that had done so much to forge a united Germany. Later, Germany would develop pride in the German navy that Tirpitz turned from a small coastal defence force into a powerful unit capable of challenging the formidable Royal Navy. The massive expansion of the German navy was a fine example of Germany's booming economy, strong grasp of design and the development of the most up to date technology available (Fulbrook, 1991, p. 3). German military strength and the rise of her naval power were a source of national pride, yet internationally the French wanted revenge for 1870, whilst the British and the Russians were wary of German intentions (Roberts, 1996, p.401).

1914 – The Failure to achieve a quick victory

When Bismarck had been Chancellor he had been careful to keep France isolated. However, the Kaiser's quest to increase German power and prestige meant that Russia and Britain became closer to France. The Kaiser's poor diplomacy and lack of tact meant that Germany had to fight on two fronts. The German military planned for a quick victory in the war in the west to avoid prolonged war on two fronts, although the breaching of Belgian neutrality caused Britain to join the war. However the Germans gained a crushing victory against the Russians at Tannenberg and the Eastern Front, yet were unable to finish the war on the Western Front in 1914 (Colvin, 2004, p.244).

There had been some demonstrations in favour of German involvement in the First World War. The nationalists played up the numbers in favour whilst the political left wing played down the numbers of people that were strongly in favour of the war. German newspapers at the time noticed that those most in favour were 'middle class students and young professional men' (Stevenson, 2004, p. 39).

Despite rapid advances in the war the Germans were eventually stopped by the French and British, which would mean a long war. The German invasion of Belgium had brought Britain into the First World War, which meant that the German army had to gain victory before the Royal Navy blockade starved Germany into submission (Kennedy, 1976 p. 246). The myth of the greatness of the German army had not been broken in 1914; after all it had almost gained a swift victory in the war. The stunning victory at Tannenberg had produced two new heroes in the form of Hindenburg and Ludendorff who both became leading figures in the conduct of the war, as well as having a great deal of political influence. Neither side was able to break the stalemate on the Western front in 1915, although the Germans helped Turkey to stop the allied offensive in Gallipoli. From an early stage in the First World War the German government realised the importance of propaganda in maintaining both military and civilian morale. Any successes were exaggerated, set backs were either not mentioned at all or their significance was played down (Bourne, Liddle & Whitehead, 2001, p.49).

Verdun, Jutland and the Somme – the stalemate continues

The German army put all its hopes of victory into the major offensive against Verdun in 1916; Falkenhayn aimed to break French morale. The German government presented the Verdun offensive as a victory due to the French sustaining heavier losses. The attack on Verdun brought forward the British led offensive on the Somme. For the Germans, the Somme helped to create the myth that the German army could not be defeated. The defences of the Hindenburg line were formidable and a massive artillery barrage proved ineffective. The barely touched or harmed German defenders decimated the advancing British and French soldiers. Allied failure to make a breakthrough in the Somme helped to keep Germany fighting and also kept civilian morale high (Bourne, Liddle & Whitehead, 2001, p. 459). However, the most important battle of 1916 was at sea, the battle of Jutland. The Germans claimed victory as they had inflicted heavier losses upon the Royal Navy. The German government did not make it public that Jutland had almost been a disaster. The Germans had planned to reduce the superior numbers of the Royal Navy by isolating units from the main British fleet and sinking them all. Instead of that, the Germans met up with the entire Grand Fleet. Only nightfall and the cautious British admirals prevented disaster. The main German naval threat came from its submarine force, and the crews of the High Seas Fleet proved more of a threat to the German government than the British (Kennedy, 1976, p.247).

German Propaganda

During the First World War the German government controlled what newspapers could publish, thus the press did not usually publicise official casualty or fatality figures, discuss food and fuel shortages or mention anti-war protests. The German government vetted all public theatre or musical performances, whilst the country's 7,500 cinemas could only show German made films that were considered patriotic. Hollywood films were banned as culturally unsound even before the United States entered the war. German cinemas did show newsreel footage of the war from 1917, yet that footage was restricted in the images that were shown. Germany produced less propaganda articles or posters than Britain or France. German news coverage and propaganda lacked effectiveness compared to British propaganda (Stevenson, 2004, p.277).

For the fist year of the war many propaganda feature films were made that unrealistically portrayed the war and was generally considered ineffective. From the end of 1915 German film makers reverted to more popular film genres such as detective stories and Westerns. Feature films were generally shown after newsreel footage of the war that would give people limited perspective on conditions at the front. The government hoped cinemas would show footage that did not show bad news from the front. Ludendorff did not start to control newsreel footage and feature films until 1917 (Chickering, 1998, p.137).

Not only was German propaganda promoted through the press and the cinema, postcards and posters were produced that urged civilians to contribute to the war effort by investing in war loans and government bonds. The German government was hampered due to the political parties being unable to agree upon the country's war aims, there was disagreement as to whether they were fighting a war of containment or fighting for financial or territorial gains (Stevenson, 2004, p.277).

The German government seemed merely to want to tell the German media what it could not print or broadcast that it missed the opportunity to ensure that propaganda and information was presented in the most effective manner. The government left the decision of how to present information about the progress of the war to the newspaper editors. The style of writing and presentation of newspapers were adapted to the tastes of the people that brought the newspapers. To a certain extent official information and propaganda was able to disguise bad news from the front yet perhaps it was only effective due to wishful thinking or naivety on the home front. German propaganda and censorship however could not hide food shortage form the German people, those that were not in the army or did not live in agricultural areas had to make do with 50% less food than in 1914 (Stevenson, 2004, p.279). As well as food shortages there were fuel shortages, especially of coal. Coal was the main domestic and industrial fuel, as well as being used for fuelling trains. The lack of coal hampered arms production, slowed down the transport of munitions and food supplies. For civilians being cold added to the misery of hunger (Chickering, 1998 p. 140).

Royal Navy blockade, shortages and the Spring Offensive

Food and fuel shortages became increasingly detrimental due to poor weather. The bitterly cold winter of 1916 was followed by an unusually wet spring in 1917 that badly affected the potato crop. The potato shortage was critical, as the potato was a staple part of human and livestock diets. The potato crop dropped by 50% between 1916 and 1917; all cereal crops dropped by 30% with milk production falling by the same percentage. Enough alternative food such as turnips could
not be grown to prevent the official rations being drastically reduced,

or the spread of malnutrition. In an effort to prolong the war effort food, fuel, and transport were used by the military before anything was available to the civilian population (Chickering, 1998, p. 142).

It was also difficult to cover up increasing political divisions over the conduct of the war. The divisions within the Social Democrats would have the most political significance. Perhaps foolishly the government had not banned public discussions about national war aims, or whether Germany should find ways to end the war through peace talks. The government could not hide the splits of the Social Democratic Party (SPD) either. The most left wing of the Social Democratic splinter groups, the USPD was very outspoken about Germany's chances of winning the war and called for ending it as soon as possible. The majority of the SPD membership stayed loyal to the party leadership, which supported the continuation of a defensive war. The majority SPD called upon the government to agree peace terms during 1917 an act that meant German nationalists regarded them as traitors. The German military later picked the SPD to lead the civilian government that ended the war, making the SPD scapegoats for German defeat in the process (Spalding, 1999, p.67). During the course of the First World War, German newspapers changed in size and in the actual print types used. The newspapers became smaller, more tabloid size rather than broad sheet size, and previously ornate gothic style fonts were made simpler to read. Some believed that these changes made propaganda more effective as people found newspapers more visually attractive, whilst others counter that written content rather than graphic design was the most important part of propaganda. Although smaller newspapers with simpler print types may have pleased readers such changes owed more to shortages of paper than altered graphic design or attempts to make propaganda more effective. An area German propaganda was highly effective in was the already mentioned use of postcards and posters to persuade people to invest in war loans (Stevenson, 2004, p.279).

The German government had great confidence that its submarines or U-boats could get Britain out of the war by breaking its Atlantic supply lines. At first the German navy had stuck to the rules of war, only naval ships were sunk on sight, merchant ships were inspected and all crews were usually evacuated before sinking the ships. The Royal Navy responded by arming merchant ships and using 'Q' ships, these were warships disguised as merchant ships to sink unsuspecting U-boats (a successful strategy that broke international law). U-boat commanders retaliated by sinking ships they believed to be armed or carrying munitions. The German government convinced the German public that its U-boats were providing heroic services and could even win the war. The U-boats caused controversy following the sinking of the liner Lusitania in May 1915 with the loss of over 1,000 lives, including many Americans. German propaganda that the Lusitania was carrying munitions was not widely accepted. The sink on sight policy was dropped to prevent the United States entering the war (Rayner & Stapley, 2006, p.105). The Germans returned to unrestricted submarine warfare in 1917, which caused heavy shipping losses. The negative consequence was that it altered American public opinion to support entry into the war (Hobsbawm, 1994, p.28).

Despite the failure of the U-boat campaign to eliminate Britain from the First World War, the Germans still had chances to win the war. The collapse of the Tsarist regime in Russia presented the German military with opportunities to win the war before the United States could intervene decisively. The Russian Provisional Government carried on fighting against Germany, although the October Revolution that brought the Bolsheviks to power effectively ended the fighting on the Eastern front (Bullock, 1991, p.69). The Russian exit from the war allowed Hindenburg and Ludendorff to transfer army units from the Eastern to the Western Front for the Spring offensive of 1918 (which they knew was their last chance to win the war). There was the drawback that part of the German army and navy became attracted to revolutionary ideas as a means to end the war and bring fundamental political changes to Germany. Subversive ideas were also spread by the army's practice of punishing strikers and militant trade unionists to the front line as punishment (Fulbrook, 1991, p.22).

Hindenburg and Ludendorff knew something that the German government's propaganda kept from the public; the spring offensive was the last throw of the dice. Although the spring offensive gave the German army its furthest advances in the West since August 1914, it failed to break the Allies and end the war. The failure of the spring offensive meant that Germany could only lose the war. Hindenburg and Ludendorff found civilian politicians to seek an armistice to end the war. They hoped that these civilians would take the blame for the defeat, which is just what happened. The same generals that failed to win the war blamed the people left to pick up the shattered pieces of Imperial Germany for their failures. Ludendorff invented the mythology of the 'stab in the back' that so undermined the Weimar Republic, whilst Hindenburg was happy to spread the myth as widely as possible (Brendon, 2000, p.9). According to Ludendorff's version of events the German army remained undefeated yet betrayed by the spineless civilian politicians. Anybody looking rationally at the factors surrounding Germany's defeat in 1918 would have argued that the Germans could never have won the war, and that to continue fighting would have been the height of stupidity. Ludendorff's misinformation and the stab in the back concept worked so well because many millions of Germans were incapable of thinking rationally as a result of unforeseen defeat and its dramatic consequences. The harshness of the Versailles settlement itself gave greater credence to the stab in the back concept, as did the official enquiry into Germany's defeat carried out by the Reichstag in1919. The Reichstag enquiry gave Hindenburg the opportunity to support and spread the stab in the back concept and have it published by the government it sought to undermine. Ludendorff meanwhile formed links with the Nazi Party, which used his myth to great affect on the road to power (Chickering, 1998, p. 190).

Germany's defeat came as a bitter shock to the majority of the German population as the government's strict censorship of bad news and its attempts at propaganda had convinced the majority of German people that defeat was not possible or indeed likely in the near future. Propaganda and censorship made it appear that Germany was in a stronger position than was actually the case. Government bulletins had deceived people into believing that the sacrifices and losses would be worth it once victory had been achieved.

The bulletins gave an ultimately false impression that German victory was at hand. This was especially the case when the spring offensive made its initial gains. If the majority of the population had not believed wartime propaganda then the myth of the 'stab in the back' would not have gained so much currency in subsequent years after the war (Bourne, Liddle & Whitehead, 2001, p.460).

The truth was that the First World War exhausted Germany, the modernity of its army, navy and its weak allies, inefficient organisation, and the effects of the Royal Navy blockade nullified industry. The German army and the navy were affected by Communist and revolutionary impulses. The German army's morale was lowered as a result of the spring offensives, soldiers found out that the Allied armies were better fed and equipped than they were (Brendon, 2000, p.8). The army was broken after August 1918 and in non-stop retreat. It had not been defeated, although the arrival of large numbers of American troops and the surrender of Austria meant that defeat was inevitable (Holmes, 1999 p.213). The 'stab in the back' myth had no basis in reality, yet it would endure long enough to severely undermine the viability of the Weimar Republic due to millions of Germans believing it (Fulbrook, 1991, p.23).

Chapter 2 Mythology & Modernity during the Weimar Republic

Some of Imperial Germany's most gifted artists, architects, and writers had fought in the First World War. Although some of them had held left wing political opinions, they had not avoided military service or conscription. Amongst the influential modernists that served in the war was the painter Paul Klee. Paul Klee went on to survive the conflict, whilst his fellow artists Franz Marc and August Macke were killed in action. Marc and Macke had both been talented modernist painters. They had been in a group with Wassily Kandinsky they had decided to call 'Der Blaue Reiter' or in English, The Blue Rider. This small group of artists favoured a strand of modernity referred to as abstraction (Faerna, 2000 p. 8). It has been argued that the experiences of military service had the affect of radicalising those that returned from the front. In the case of Germany, her veterans were drawn towards either the rabidly nationalist ring wing groups such as the Nazi party, or they were drawn towards the revolutionary left. Amidst the debris of a war shattered country the old monarchy was replaced by the Weimar Republic. As a matter of coincidence the centre of excellence for the modernists in Weimar era Germany, the Bauhaus school was also founded in Weimar during 1919 (Hobsbawm, 1994 p. 179). In many respects the founders of the Bauhaus school had similar political, social, and ethical ideologies to those that had drafted the constitution of the Weimar Republic. Like the architects of the Weimar Republic, the founders of the Bauhaus favoured modernity, cultural diversity, and they were internationalist in outlook (James, 2003 p. 85). All students at the Bauhaus had to complete a foundation year in which they were given a taster of all the subjects that were available at the school. After that foundation year students, or apprentices as they were termed went on to study their specialist subjects. This approach was hoped to give all students an overall style and to link altogether rather than graduates just viewing themselves as designers, architects, or painters (Weimar Source Book, p. 430).

A New Beginning?

History has certainly not been kind to the Weimar Republic, Germany's first taste of liberal democracy that was detested by millions of Germans, as well as being beset by major political and economic weaknesses particularly after the Great Depression. The collapse of the monarchy had allowed the Weimar Republic to be created to the decidedly inauspicious background of military defeat, an enforced peace treaty and political unrest at home. The optimism of pre-war Imperial Germany had been shattered by the time the First World War had finished (James, 2003, p.73). The Weimar Republic had a very liberal constitution with left wing and centre parties supporting the new system. The Weimar Republic was not at first accepted by the Communists or right wing nationalist parties. The new German state lacked the economic dynamism of Imperial Germany, especially as the Ruhr Valley industry output was harnessed to the French economy. The Germans protested about the reparations enforced upon them by the Treaty of Versailles. The Versailles settlement was intended to strip Germany of the power to wage war again, the army was reduced to 100,000 men, and the high command was abolished. The German navy was reduced to a weak coastal defence force banned from having submarines. Germany was also banned from having an airforce. The Allies had hoped to break militarism in Germany, yet only caused resentment amongst the German people. Resentment of the Versailles settlement fuelled dislike of the Weimar Republic, although the government could not have rejected the treaty. Germany simply did not have the military, human, or economic resources to have carried on fighting which was why Ludendorff had brought civilians into the government in the first place, to use as fall guys for the army's failure to win the war (Shirer, 1988, p.32).

The Allies could have helped the Weimar Republic survive by making the Versailles Settlement less punitive. Germans of all political persuasions were angry about having to sign a treaty that blamed Germany for the war, forced Germany to pay reparations to the Allies, whilst seeking to prosecute the Kaiser and army commanders for war crimes. The German government could not refuse to sign the treaty, although it did leak information to foreign newspapers that might be sympathetic to its arguments. Reparations, the socalled war guilt clause combined with the desire that the

Kaiser should not be punished meant 'even left wing republicans were incensed'. Fortunately for the German government the Kaiser was in exile in the Netherlands so they did not have to face the consequences of extraditing him (Henig, 1998, p. 19). Hitler was the strongest advocate of overthrowing the Weimar Republic as it was the unpatriotic government of the 'November Criminals' that had betrayed Germany (Bullock, 1991, p. 97).

The Stab in the Back and Instability

The strong beliefs that Germany had been betrayed by the way in which the First World War had been ended led to impulses to remember all the dead even though circumstances conspired against the survivors that came back from the fighting. Monuments were built across the country to honour all the Germans killed in the First World War. Perhaps the most spectacular example was the Tannenberg Monument, which marked the German victory over the Russians in August 1914. It was a monument to a victory rather than a memorial to a defeat. Later Hitler decided that the Tannenberg Monument made a fitting tomb for Hindenburg. The Soviet Army showed its disapproval of the monument by having it demolished after the Second World War (Watkins, 2005, p.601).

However fragile the political and economic situation was in the Weimar era, Germany was certainly not a cultural or artistic backwater. In fact, Germany during the Republican period gained an international renown for its cultural and artistic achievements. Some of these cultural and artistic trends had existed before the First World War; others such as the Bauhaus School most closely linked with Walter Gropius flourished in this period (Fulbrook, 1991, p.39). Much of the cultural diversity witnessed during the Weimar Republic fits into the concepts of modernity. Walter Gropius, Thomas Mann, and Arnold Schonberg were notable members of the German modernist avant-garde who got their best opportunities to fully express themselves after the First World War (Hobsbawm, 1994, p.179).

German avant-garde modernism was influenced by two American imports after the First World War, cinematic films, and jazz music.

The Weimar Republic had a flourishing filmmaking sector, although it could not match the production levels or profits generated by Hollywood. Hollywood studios, especially Universal Studios liked to use ideas from relatively unknown German films, such as Frankenstein. Even before the Nazi's took power and repressed the degenerate elements of modernity; German technicians and filmmakers could always find work in Hollywood. Gropius and the Bauhaus linked itself with jazz music, which they regarded as the height of modernity in musical terms. The right wing politicians and extreme nationalists disliked jazz due to its Black American origin, as much as for its musical merits (Hobsbawm, 1994, pp.184-85).

The Bauhaus School membership was almost entirely made up of left wing sympathisers who preferred the new republic to the old monarchy. The Bauhaus was established to fulfil objectives that related to graphic design, art, and architecture that arguably had political undertones. Bruno Taut argued that there were no unifying features in art at that time, yet architecture could provide the basis for artists, painters, sculptors, and graphic designers to work constructively together (Weimar Source Book, p. 430). Gropius was adamant that the Bauhaus should be force for driving forward artistic, design, and architectural achievements. The overall aim of the Bauhaus ' was to bring together all creative effort into one whole to reunify all disciplines of practical art' (Weimar Source Book, p. 435). Gropius wanted the Bauhaus to differ from the Werkbund in that architectural projects and graphic designs should not be exclusively created for the wealthy or businesses but for ordinary people. Art and design should not be confined to those that could afford to pay for it. Gropius reasoned that if modern technology allowed for the mass production of consumer products it could also be adopted for the mass production of graphic design as well as buildings. Gropius also supported the concept of public housing projects (Gropius, p. 115).
The Social Democrats retained their previous popularity but the new Weimar Republic actually allowed it a share of power. The greater freedoms that were allowed under the Republican regime would mean that the Bauhaus and other centres of German modernity were not only linked with Socialism or Marxism, they were also linked with Germany's moral degeneration. Places where new culture was

stronger, especially Berlin, were frequently resented for moral decadence and politically subversive views. The Bauhaus also tried to change the print types used in German newspapers and their own printed material. This was partly to make the graphic design better to look at as well as to save resources which traditional print types used more of (Fulbrook, 1991, p.41).

For instance, Lyonell Feininger taught at the Bauhaus, yet had previously been a cartoonist that had gained a reputation for producing hard hitting political satire in his newspaper cartoons. Whilst working for the Bauhaus Feininger went on to become a highly skilled painter and woodcutter. His work reflected that the influence of the Cubist movement remained strong throughout his career (. Wassily Kandinsky had been a founding member of the 'Blaue Reiter' before the First World War forced his return to his native Russia. Whilst at the Bauhaus, Kandinsky did some of his finest work most notably the 'Kleine Welten' of 1922. He broadened his artistic horizons, whilst using his skills as a graphic designer to produce stage sets and theatrical costumes. Laszlo Moholy-Nagy came up with some innovative photographic techniques that later became widely used in journalistic graphic design. These techniques produced photographic quality pictures without the need to use a camera which Moholy–Nagy referred to as photograms. Moholy – Nagy became a film producer, as well as further developing photograms to be incorporated into printed text (Crystal, 1998 p. 652).

A Progressive yet unpopular Republic

Dislike of the new democratic Germany was not just confined to extreme nationalist groups, teachers, civil servants, as well as the Catholic and Protestant churches were suspicious if not downright hostile towards the Weimar Republic. The political, social and ethical decadence of the Weimar Republic came to a head in 1923. This year was when the French occupied the Ruhr Valley and also when Germany was devastated by hyperinflation. Hyperinflation brought misery to millions of ordinary Germans; it made wages, savings, and pensions worthless (Brendon, 2000, pp.29-30). Some businesses and the large land owning estates increased their fortunes due to the hyperinflation allowing them the opportunity to pay off their debts with worthless money (Bullock, 1991, p. 95). Millions turned in desperation towards the Communists, but also for the first time the Nazi party. Hyperinflation was the event, which also saw Adolf Hitler brought to national attention, after the failed putsch in Munich during November 1923. Hitler skilfully used his trial to publicly express the aims of the Nazi party. Germany's severe economic problems also prompted American recovery packages that gave the Weimar Republic the appearance of political and economic stability (Brendon, 2000, pp.29-30).

Domestically, stability seemed to be achieved under the guidance of the foreign minister Gustav Stressman. The desire for stability and order amongst the majority of Germans was reflected in the election of the elderly Hindenburg as President. Under the constitution of the Weimar Republic the President held considerable powers. However, Germany's apparent recovery meant that many believed that hyperinflation, high unemployment and political extremism were things of the past. Perhaps only Adolf Hitler believed that hard times lay ahead (Shirer, 1988, p.118). The period between 1923 and 1929 was the period in which modernity had a greater impact upon political, social and ethical ideologies of graphic design than mythology did. However, although modernity had a strong hold on the artistic and cultural aspects of German socialists and radicals, it was mythology that still had a strong political and ethical hold on the beliefs of many Germans, particularly those with right wing, Christian, or nationalist opinions. These people in desperation would turn to the Nazi party in the wake of the Great Depression (Brendon, 2000, p.30).

The Bauhaus quickly gained an excellent reputation for the high quality of its teaching, its eminent teaching staff and the quality of the commissions it undertook. From its start the Bauhaus had strong links with the Soviet Union, some of its staff were actually Russian, most notably Wassily Kandinsky. The Bauhaus was established with the express intention of promoting modernity and progresses in architecture and art (www.bauhaus/archiv) .

The Bauhaus showed its progressive and modernist credentials with the buildings it designed. The school even carried out commissions outside of Germany. Buildings were not the only projects that the Bauhaus worked on. Some projects reflected the left-wing beliefs of the school. For instance, Mies van Der Rohe completed a memorial for the murdered Marxist revolutionaries Karl Liebneckt and Rosa Luxemburg, erected in Berlin for the Communist party (Hobsbawm, 1994, p.187). Rohe's commemorative monument to Liebneckt and Luxemburg was an 'abstract rectilinear composition of twister clinker brick, enlivened with a hammer and sickle (Watkins, 2005, p.598).

The Bauhaus school moved from its original base in Weimar to a brand new campus at Dessau during 1925. The actual buildings of the Dessau campus designed by Walter Gropius himself were prime examples of functional modernity being constructed in steel and glass. Surprisingly enough given the skills and experience of its academic staff, the Bauhaus school did not have a separate architectural department until 1928. The designs that came from the Bauhaus school were primary examples of modernity influenced by movements such as De stijl and Russian constructivism (Bayer, 1999, p.23). Walter Gropius' own designs were heavily influenced by Cubism. The cubist style adopted was pragmatic, unpretentious, and yet modernist. For Gropius such a style was a continuation of his designs before the First World War, for instance, the Fagus factory completed in 1911(Pevsner, 1995, p.176).

The Bauhaus School

Walter Gropius, Mies van der Rohe, and their contemporaries at the Bauhaus raised the profile of modernist architecture and graphic design beyond Germany, even though the number of modernist buildings in Germany was cut short by the demise of the Weimar Republic (Ghirardo, 1996, p.9). Indeed, Walter Gropius was so committed to modernism in architecture that he dropped the studying of historical buildings from the Curriculum at the Bauhaus. That was an approach that was adopted in other countries, especially the United States (Ghirardo, 1996, p.17).

The Bauhaus school did not confine its work and projects to the construction of modernist inspired buildings and pieces of art. The avant garde influences that had been noticeable in German graphic design and art before the First World War were dropped from the graphic designs and teachings of the Bauhaus school. Here was a school of graphic design and architecture that used graphic design for essentially pragmatic projects rather than paintings or art. The Bauhaus experimented with and pioneered the use of more advanced graphic designs for advertising posters and displays, which had political implications as well as commercial ones, in that propaganda or campaigns could have a stronger impact on voters as well as consumers. Walter Gropius tried his hand at designing cars or at least their interiors and exteriors (leaving the mechanical side of things to engineers) others designed aircraft seats for the emerging airliner services. The Bauhaus even did graphic design for the government, designing high denomination bank notes during the hyperinflation of 1923. Perhaps they had to leave extra room for a few more zeros as inflation had usually risen in between the designs being completed and the bank notes being printed (Hobsbawm 1994 p. 186).

The modernist influenced graphic designs for those followers of the modernity approach to graphic design critically acclaimed the innovative campus buildings of the Bauhaus school. However the modernist designs of steel and glass construction of the original Bauhaus campus buildings in Weimar were not that popular with everybody. The local authority of Weimar made no secret of its dislike of the Bauhaus school and the modernity of its graphic design. It was not just the graphic design of the Bauhaus school that was not trusted, what it taught also came under suspicion of being politically, socially, and ethically unsound. Poor relations with the Weimar local authority greatly contributed towards the decision to move the entire campus to Dessau in 1925. The Bauhaus school then decided to move the campus for a third and final time to Berlin. The move to Berlin was intended to raise the profile of the Bauhaus school. Berlin of course, was supposed to have a more liberal set of political, social, and ethical values than the more conservative or traditionally cultured cities of Weimar and Dessau. Unfortunately, the accession of the Nazi party to power meant that the move to Berlin was a short lived one. For the new regime was determined to close the Bauhaus school down and did so within a year of gaining power (Bayer, 1999 p. 23).

The founders of the Weimar Republic had intended to fundamentally change German culture as a means of transforming its politics and its society. They intended to replace the mythology concerning the German nation being a great power, which through military and economic power could bully other nations and deny its citizens freedom. The Weimar Republic was intended to bring Germany into the modernist world as a progressive democratic and pluralistic state. Imperial Germany had universal male suffrage and political parties, although the power held by the Kaiser meant that it was not a genuine democracy. In the Weimar Republic there was universal adult suffrage. Everybody over 20 years of age was given the vote and unlike Imperial Germany each person just had votes of equal value, rather than there been differing numbers of votes dependent on occupation and income. The German Republic was aiming towards egalitarian and modernity. However, in reality the Weimar Republic never lived up to the expectations of its founders. The German Republic had too many detractors for its own good, detractors awaiting the opportunity to subvert the Weimar Constitution. Perhaps the weakest link in the Weimar Constitution was the electoral system used, it was the most accurate Proportional Representation system adopted at that point. The problem was that the Proportional Representation system allowed extremist parties to get into the Reichstag and it made it harder for the constitutional parties to provide stable and effective governments. The Weimar Republic had more than twenty governments during its mostly troubled fourteen years of existence (Burns, 1995, p.57).

The modernist and democratic mission of the Weimar Republic was always fragile and the effects of the Great Depression proved fatal; for the Great Depression presented opportunities for the one person capable of destroying the Weimar Republic, Adolf Hitler (Shirer, 1988, p.).

Chapter 3 Mythology, Modernity and the Third Reich

The End of Freedom

The accession of Adolf Hitler and the Nazi party to power had almost immediate consequences for those in Germany that favoured modernity in graphic design, as well as for those that had left wing political and social ideological beliefs. The Nazi party's accession to power also had immediate consequences for those people that happened to be Jewish, such as Paul Klee. Official discrimination and unofficial intimidation forced thousands of German Jews to go into exile; Paul Klee included amongst them. Adolf Hitler had no time for modernist architects and artists, whose work he considered morally degenerate and politically subversive (Speer, 1970, p.60). Hitler was not opposed to modernity as such; he was opposed to those people that used modernity as a means to advance their progressive, socialist, and even Marxist beliefs. When used in that particular context, modernity stood for everything that the Nazi party detested. Modernity in graphic design, architecture or art promoted values such as internationalism and socialism. Modernist schools such as Bauhaus were frequently accused by the Nazi party of promoting 'Bolshevik Culture' so it was no surprise that it was expedient by most members of the Bauhaus school, as well as the actual school itself to leave the Third Reich (Faerna, 2000, p.8).

Hitler may have used mythology and democracy as the primary means to gain power, yet that did not mean that he was against using modern technologies or techniques to achieve his political and social objectives. Hitler was highly adept at public speaking, both at rallies and in radio broadcasts. Hitler's campaign for the presidential election of 1932 was textbook electioneering. The Hitler over Germany campaign brought the Nazi leader millions of extra votes and gave him a respectable second place behind Hindenburg (Rees, 1997, p.41). If the Nazis use of the media, propaganda, and the newest technology were astute on the road to power, it would be even more accomplished once they held power. Control of state owned media, the strict censorship of the press, combined with control of the education system meant that Goebbels was able to spread Nazi mythology and ideology to the entire population (Rees, 1997, p.75).

Speer and the Nazi use of Modernity

Hitler had grandiose plans to profoundly alter Germany's architecture to reflect the glory and the power of the thousand years that the Third Reich was supposed to last. The man he chose to lead the architectural revolution was a young relatively unknown architect, Albert Speer. Speer was a classically trained architect whose designs had caught Hitler's attention. Speer designed the new chancellery building in Berlin. Speer did not use modernity for any of the buildings that he planned and built for Hitler. Speer was to plan more buildings than he ever got around to having built. The Second World War would delay and then prevent Hitler's ambitions to rebuild many German cities with a classically or mythological inspired graphic design. Ultimately the lead for rejecting modernity in graphic design in favour of a mythological approach to art and architecture came from Adolf Hitler himself. In his memoirs Speer recounted that even government ministers such as Joseph Goebbels (and during the Second World War himself) had to be very careful about any art displays or building work carried out in case Adolf Hitler 'expressed his severe disapproval'. Hitler tried to ensure that his tastes in graphic design and art decided the forms that were tolerated in the Third Reich (Speer, 1970 p. 60).

Hitler planned that he would commission Speer to redesign much of Berlin, plans that were put on hold due to the start of the Second World War. Hitler found another use for Speer; he was the man responsible for the design of the Nuremburg rallies. The Nuremburg rallies were the ultimate way of demonstrating Nazi mythology of 'Ein Volke, Ein Reich, Ein Fuhrer' as well as Germany's renewed prestige in the war (Speer, 1970, p.61). If anybody doubted the Nazis ability to produce sophisticated propaganda they only had to watch the film 'Triumph of the Will' which brilliantly showcased Speer's Cathedral of Light' as the backdrop to the Nazi Party Congress of 1934 (Bullock, 1991, p.385).

Hitler and Architecture

Hitler was obsessed with architecture; he wanted massive
monuments built that would last for thousands of years. In such
circumstances the scale of buildings were more important than the
style. Classical or neo-classical designs were adopted, as those were
the designs that Hitler preferred. Modernist buildings of glass and
steel were not much good as the intention was to design buildings
that would have lasted for thousands of years as testament to the
greatness of the Third Reich (Bullock, 1991, p.429). Speer's major
architectural achievements were the New Chancellery building and
the critically acclaimed Olympic stadium, both situated in Berlin.
The Second World War curtailed any further large-scale construction
(Watkins, 2005, p. 601).

The Nazi regime instigated programmes and policies to profoundly
alter the cultural, ethical and racial purity of the German nation to fit
in with its distorted views of German nationality. Graphic design in
the Third Reich had to conform to the dominant political, social and
ethical ideologies, or face severe restrictions upon its practice. The
Nazi regime was opposed to most of those that worked on graphic
design due to their political, social and ethical beliefs differing from
those of the regime. Adolf Hitler and Joseph Goebbels were too
astute in the use of propaganda and public relations to believe that
the Third Reich could do without graphic design. Whilst the artistic,
cultural and graphic design skills of people like Gropius, Van der
Rohe and Klee were beyond doubt, the same thing could not be said
about their political, social and ethical beliefs. The Nazi regime was
confident that it did not need the services of such talented graphic
designers as the regime believed that it could find people to fulfil
similar functions that were politically reliable, as well as being
racially and culturally pure enough to be part of the new Germany.
The Third Reich did not want graphic designers to be producing
politically suspect and morally degenerate art of designs. The Nazi
regime did allow an exhibition of degenerate art in 1937 yet many
artists, graphic designers, and architects did not feel comfortable or
safe contributing works or exhibits towards it. Instead graphic
design was adapted to serve the needs of the Third Reich in its
campaigns to restore the political, economic, cultural and military

greatness of Germany, destroyed by Imperial Germany's defeat in the First World War and by the degenerate nature of the Weimar Republic (Hobsbawm, 1994, p.39).

Artist turned Dictator

Adolf Hitler was a man that took a great deal of interest in art, graphic design, and architecture.
Indeed, Hitler had originally intended to become a great artist, as well as developing a keen interest in architecture and the mythological based operas of Richard Wagner. Indeed after politics, and his obsession with the racial purity of the German nation, art, architecture, and music were amongst his passions. However, Hitler failed to make the grade as either an artist or as an architect. In his youth he seemed to lose his way in life, until leaving his native Austria to serve in the far more effective German army during the First World War, this gave him a purpose in life. Hitler was despondent as any native born German about the military defeat and profound national humiliation that Germany was forced to endure in November 1918. He readily accepted the mythology of 'the stab in the back' as a central part of the Nazi party rhetoric. Adolf Hitler may only have been a third rate artist or architect whose loss as an artist was insignificant, yet his skills as a politician and his use of propaganda were highly pronounced if not exactly conventional. After the failed putsch of November 1923 Hitler used constitutional means to attempt to gain power, aside from the street fighting used by the brown shirted SA storm-troopers to intimidate political opponents, especially the Communists. As a party the Nazi party seemed a long way from power before the Great Depression hit the Weimar Republic with devastating force. Through carefully organised posters and above all his public speaking, Hitler persuaded enough Germans that he was the German nation's saviour to get him in the position to gain power when he was given the opportunity to do so. During Hitler's rise to power the rewards of well-designed posters and public broadcasting became apparent to the Nazi party leadership. Hitler's speaking style was particularly effective at gaining support at party rallies, the back drop of which became spectacular once the Nazi Party gained power (Bullock, 1991 p. 429).

For left wing intellectuals, academics, artists and architects the Nazi's gaining power was disastrous in terms of their career prospects and even their personal safety. As the party tightened its grip upon power its opponents had stark choices, they could go into exile, they could stay in Germany and resist the regime, or they could chose to remain in Germany and conform to the Nazi regime's wishes. Initially, many Germans were happy to have their freedom restricted by a regime that promised to restore the country's military and economic strength, whilst ending political stability. Hitler was fortunate enough to gain intimidated power due to the burning down of the Reichstag and the timely death of Hindenburg, which allowed the regime to use enabling acts and for Hitler to adopt the title of Fuhrer. As already mentioned, Hitler was a man that understood and excelled at the used of propaganda and public images to gain or maintain popular support (Bullock, 1991 p. 430).

The regime was also able to quickly suppress its political rivals, especially the Social Democrats and the Communists, as well as taking measures against German Jewish communities. Joseph Goebbels and Albert Speer ably assisted Hitler in presenting the public image and celebrating the successes of the regime. Drastically reduced unemployment, the autobahns, the staging of the 1936 Berlin Olympics and renewed optimism were potent symbols of the regime's success. Hitler had not used any of the graphic designers linked with Bauhaus school for such ambitious building projects, apart from their political, social and ethical unsuitability, most of them had already had the good sense to have gone into exile. The Nazi regime used both mythology and modernity in graphic design on a pragmatic basis, depending upon its need or objectives during any given time. The autobahns, the Olympic stadiums, or even the Volkswagen Beetle could all be seen as very public examples of modernity in graphic design. Such projects brought benefits such as improving German transport infrastructure, and increasingly preparing the German people towards war. The staging of the Nazi party rallies are another example of the regime manipulating aspects of graphic design to publicly show its power and prestige. Rallies were held with the background of giant swastikas, large gold coloured German eagles and smartly dressed

SS units.

The rallies were also an opportunity to showcase Germany's re-emerging military power as the Nazi regime defied the Versailles Settlement through rearmament. As well as being meant for domestic German audiences, the Nazi party was used to demonstrate Germany's increasing military strength for the benefit of foreign governments and populations. Hitler wanted to show that the regime was getting stronger to reduce internal opposition and gain diplomatic concessions. The main use for modernist graphic design in the Third Reich was linked with German rearmament and the development of new weapons. Propaganda was successfully used to maintain public support for Hitler's foreign policy as he managed to regain the Rhineland, achieve union with Austria and obtain the Sudetenland from Czechoslovakia without going to war. For Hitler the start of the Second World War was more successful than could ever been anticipated, reinforcing the mythology which presented him as being the saviour of Germany. However, the alliance between Britain, the United States, and the Soviet Union ended the Third Reich in the most catastrophic way possible for the German people (Bullock, 1991 p. 431).

The influence and work of modernist graphic design based upon the principles of the Bauhaus school did not stop with the end of the Weimar Republic or the closure of the actual Bauhaus school in Berlin. The leading lights of the Bauhaus school went into exile to carry on working and designing. Gropius and Van der Rohe, amongst other leading members of the Bauhaus went on to have distinguished academic and architectural careers in the United States. Walter Gropius for instance worked at Harvard University and on various architectural projects. Van der Rohe went on to design a series of prestigious skyscraper projects. Therefore, working and living in exile increased the influence of the Bauhaus school's former members on modernist graphic design in Western Europe and North America. The influence of the Bauhaus can be seen on many skyscrapers and office blocks in major cities such as Chicago and New York (Ghirardo, 1996, p.17).

Chapter 4 Mythology, Modernity and the Soviet Union

The world's first Communist state

The Soviet Union was a state, which was founded upon the principles of Marxist-Leninist ideology, and whose regime was intent upon spreading those principles to all its citizens and to exporting revolution to other countries. After winning the Russian Civil War the Bolshevik regime consolidated its political position as a one party state that Lenin referred to as the 'Dictatorship of the Proletariat.' The Soviet regime used graphic design as a means to consolidate its hold on power as well as means of exporting Marxist-Leninist revolution to any country that was susceptible to it, such as Germany (Bullock, 1991, p. 431).

Modernity and Soviet Propaganda

In the Soviet Union once power was secured the Communist Party leadership was the final judge of what was politically, socially, and culturally acceptable and what was unacceptable. The Communist Party made those decisions due there been nobody else in the Soviet Union was capable or permitted to do so. Graphic design was an important element of consolidating the Soviet regime, via propaganda, education, and the construction of housing and industrial plants that were intended to end Soviet backwardness and develop its economy and infrastructure. In the words of Lenin 'the Communist Party is capable of unifying, educating and organising a vanguard of the proletariat' (Bullock, 1991 p. 86).

The Soviet Union was a revolutionary state whose leadership had initially hoped to spread Communist revolution across the globe. For a time they were hopeful about the position in Germany, although the Sparticus Revolt and the self styled Soviet Republic of Bavaria were crushed by a combination of the army and ex-servicemen in right wing paramilitary groups such as the Freikorps. The Soviet leadership soon realised that it needed a combination of mythology and modernity to secure its hold on power using propaganda and education, extensive coercion, and rapid modernisation. The gist of the propaganda was that the Soviet Union would be the vanguard of global revolution, whilst at the same time ending the political, social and economic backwardness inherited from old Imperial Russia. The Bolsheviks believed that spreading myths about their destiny to transform the Soviet Union through state run newspapers, the modern media of cinematic films and eventually radio would help their campaigns to a Marxist-Leninist version of modernity. The heyday of Soviet film making would prove to be the 1920s when internal debate was still allowed within the Communist party and when the need to establish myths about the regime was greatest. Stalin was less keen on allowing film makers, newspaper editors, and graphic designers freedom of expression; in fact it was strictly subordinated to Stalin's objectives and plans (Kenez, 1992, p.3).

Civil War and Lenin's rule

Whilst Lenin was still alive the most potent myth the regime promoted about itself was that of 'Red October' whilst the red flag became the most graphical symbol for revolutionaries everywhere across the globe. The red flag was also universally feared in capitalist states, with the Communist parties of other countries facing repression and hatred as they were frequently regarded as being unpatriotic. As well as films, the regime used posters and cartoons to put across its messages. These were particularly effective methods of propaganda, especially when the high rates of illiteracy at the start of the 1920s are taken into account. Ending illiteracy was one of the Soviet's regime strategies for modernising such a backward country; it also offered the prospect of making the regime's propaganda more effective as more people would understand it. The Soviet regime was willing to work with certain aspects of modernity, although solely as a means to an end, the strengthening of Communism. The direction the Soviet Union might have taken, if Lenin had lived longer, has been the subject of many debates. In hindsight the 1920s would be a freer decade in terms of freedom of expression and debate, yet Lenin was definitely not interested in democratic practices. It was Lenin that constructed the Soviet state infrastructure that Stalin readily adopted towards his reign of terror as well the brutally enforced processes of collectivisation and industrialisation (Roberts, 1996 p. 488).

Soviet links with Germany

During the 1920s the Soviet Union had strong links with the modernist movement of the Weimar Republic. In the early 1920s especially after the signing of the Treaty of Rapello the relationship between the Soviet Union and the Weimar Republic was good. Both countries at that time were international outcasts. Germany gave the Soviets technical advice to help the modernisation of the Soviet economy. In return Germany was able to develop weapons and carry out research in breach of the Treaty of Versailles. The Treaty of Rapello was a pragmatic agreement rather than one based on mythology, modernity or driven by ideological considerations. German modernists mostly had an affinity towards the Soviet Union, which helps to explain why the Bauhaus had strong links with the Soviet Union. The Soviet Union was a source of work and commissions due to work becoming harder to come by in Germany because of the Great Depression and later the open hostility of the Nazi regime. Eventually the former members of the Bauhaus teaching staff were happier in the West after they went into exile, with the United States being their preferred destination (Hobsbawm, 1994 p. 186).

Graphic design as a propaganda tool

Due to the ideological nature of the Soviet regime, graphic design was a key feature of its propaganda campaigns. Soviet propaganda campaigns used posters, cartons, newspaper articles, and films to promote the regime's objectives. The propaganda messages would change depending on the contemporary Soviet policies at any given time. Stalin in particular would change government policies or tactics seemingly at a whim to maximise his personal hold on power. For instance when the New Economic Policy (NEP) with the dual strategies of collectivisation and industrialisation. The style if not the messages of Soviet propaganda remained essentially the same throughout the inter-war period. For both internal and external scrutinisers of Soviet propaganda the gist of the message was usually the same, the Soviet Union was the first Communist state and that it would be the showcase for communism. Soviet posters praised industrial workers for their hard work whilst urging them to work even harder to successfully modernise the Soviet Union. Slogans were usually featured on Soviet propaganda, as were heroes and villains such as the proletariat as opposed to the rich peasants or kulaks. For instance a poster of the early 1920s featuring industrial workers featured the following slogan: 'We have beaten the enemy by force of arms. We will earn our bread by labour. Everything for work, comrades (Spalding, 1999, pp. 62-63).

Stalin and Propaganda

Under Stalin propaganda was used to promote the processes of collectivisation and
industrialisation. These two processes were inter-linked. Collectivisation was supposed to make Soviet agriculture more efficient, allowing millions of peasants to become industrial workers in the cities, some of, which were entirely new cities constructed around factories. Higher agricultural output was intended to be exported abroad to fund industrialisation and pay for foreign machinery and experts. In the event strong resistance from the peasantry meant that agricultural production decline sharply, which led to the Soviet regime resorting to force collectivisation, and the requisition of food supplies. Stalin publicly justified the war against the kulaks as necessary for the future of the Soviet Union, although in reality it meant the elimination of the most productive agricultural workers. By the time collectivisation was completed millions had died as a result of executions, being sent to labour camps, and starvation. The Soviet regime publicly offered incentives for all workers to exceed their production quotas with the prospects of better quality public housing and even holidays to government run resorts. To exceed production quotas took excessive amounts of hard work, as the majority of quotas were unrealistically high. One miner, Alexi Stakhanov achieved celebrity status for his work achievements and was used in government propaganda posters and articles. For the more numerous workers that failed to achieve production quotas their punishment was not so widely publicised, they were frequently sent to the gulags or forced labour camps (Spalding, 1999, p.64).

The Declining Influence of Modernity

The influence of modernity in the Soviet Union started to decline as
the power of Joseph Stalin increased. For Joseph Stalin the most
important political consideration was the consolidation of his power,
policies would be changed in order to increase his authority. Aside
from the attainment of power, Joseph Stalin was interested in the use
of propaganda to fulfil his aims and to make the communists look
indispensable for the modernisation of the Soviet Union. Stalin was
happy to start the mythological based cult of Lenin after the formers'
death. That was in order to use the dead leader's image to promote
Marxist-Leninist ideals, or more accurately Stalin's version of those
ideals throughout the Soviet Union. Stalin was careful to ensure that
whatever he did was done in Lenin's name or was a policy which
appeared to be a policy that Lenin would have approved of. The cult
of Lenin was a mythology that was designed to sustain the very
existence of the Soviet Union. The cult of Lenin proved to be an
enduring mythology that lasted until the demise of the Soviet Union
itself. All subsequent Soviet leaders used Lenin's name and image to
promote their policies and agendas. Stalin went on to create a cult of
personality around himself that was closely linked to the Great
Purges and the elimination of all opposition to his regime whether
real or imagined (Bullock, 1991 p. 431).

Stalin's interest in graphic design was strictly limited to using it as a
means to increase his own personal power under the veil of
strengthening the Soviet regime. Modernity was the method for
modernising the Soviet Union as rapidly as possible. Stalin did not
particularly care about the designs of housing, schools, or factories
as long as they served the purposes they were built for. Soviet
designers had less choice about the type of building materials used
due to the low level of industrialisation combined with the loss of
output caused by the First World War and the subsequent civil war
(Roberts, 1996 p. 488).

The 1920s and 1930s did see many construction programmes carried
out in the Soviet Union, with the exception of the stations upon the
Moscow underground system the majority of new public buildings

were purely functional in nature and design. Such buildings may have inadvertently aided mythology within the Soviet Union yet they were only meant to improve modernism. After Lenin's death the use of his name and image became prevalent across the Soviet Union ranging from massive statues to badges alongside naming numerous places after him (Hobsbawm, 1994, pp.184-85).

Conclusions

Mythology and modernity have both played significant roles in the political, social and ethical ideologies linked with graphic design during the twentieth century. In the main case study of Germany, there were strong mythological and slightly weaker modernist elements in German culture and therefore in graphic design. At the beginning of the twentieth century German culture seemed to be prospering, just like its economy. Many Germans believed that their culture was superior to any other culture. Due to the way in which German unity had been achieved mythologies had developed about German military might and a strong sense of national pride. Prussia dominated Imperial Germany, which after all it had created as a united state; the Prussian King was the German Kaiser. Imperial Germany was an autocratic state, although there were democratic, socialist and modernist elements within its society. Mythology about German culture, history, and its place in the world was portrayed in art, theatre productions, and cinema films as well opera music. Prior to the First World War, Imperial Germany experienced strong growth in theatre, cinema and opera attendance, as well as rising newspaper sales. This is not to say that modernity did not exist in Germany, the Germans liked to believe that they adopted the most modern designs and technology available. The majority of artists and architects associated with the modernity movements of the Weimar Republic were already working in Imperial Germany. The Werkbund for instance, had similar aims to the Bauhaus school that it predicted and shared some of its staff in common.

The First World War was a defining moment as to whether mythology versus modernity had the most influence upon the political, social and ethical ideologies of graphic design. The German government tried to use propaganda and censorship to maintain civilian as well as military morale. To be accurate the German government mainly concentrated upon press censorship to prevent newspapers publishing negative news, rather than using the press to promote its propaganda. Although strict censorship worked as far as maintaining morale was concerned, it was not arguably as effective as the propaganda used by the British and the French. One of the side effects of strict German censorship was that it allowed the mythology to grow that the German army had not been defeated but stabbed in the back by traitors at the home front. Ludendorff's political legacies were greater than his military successes and failures, for they allowed mythology to be used to undermine the Weimar Republic and promote rabid nationalism.

In terms of graphic design the era of the golden age of the modernist approach to political, social and ethical ideologies expressed in art and architecture was during the Weimar Republic. Paramount in the modernity movement was the Bauhaus school. Walter Gropius the main founder of the Bauhaus argued that art, culture, architecture and graphic design could be taught without reference to the political, social and ethical period.

The instability of the Weimar Republic however, was a prime example of art and culture being heavily connected with political, social and economic events in a single country.
The Nazi regime intended to change the political, social, racial and ethical make up of Germany markedly to have its vision of a pure and strong German nation become a reality. Modernist graphic design was certainly not part of Nazi plans for Germany, especially by political subversives and racially impure Germans that worked for the Bauhaus. The exiles from the Bauhaus school were part of the exodus of Germany's most talented people that arguably reduced the academic and economic strength of the country. The Third Reich though was concerned with the exile of some its most capable citizens because it did not regard them as citizens at all. If anything the influence of modernity in graphic design was increased by the members of the Bauhaus school going into exile.
In the case of the Soviet Union the dominance of mythology or modernity in the area of graphic design was strictly subordinated to the wishes or aims of the Communist regime. During the 1920s Soviet graphic design was strongly influenced by modernity and had strong relationships with modernists in Germany, especially with Bauhaus school.

The Soviet government would fluctuate between mythological or modernity approach to graphic design depending on particular circumstances or objectives. For the Soviet government the main political priority was to survive in a hostile world, especially when revolution failed to take hold in other parts of Europe. The regime favoured the mythological approach to graphic design when it came to promoting the cult of Lenin after his death, as well as the cult of personality surrounding Stalin. Modernity was used in the graphic design of factories and machinery. Both mythological and modernist approaches were used in official Soviet propaganda with the attention of controlling Soviet citizens as well as trying to spread revolution abroad. The use of mythology and modernity in Soviet graphic design became less influential at the end of the 1920s once Stalin had secured his position and defeated all his rivals. The Stalin regime still had mythological and modernity approaches in propaganda during the campaigns for collectivisation, industrialisation and with the use of show trials during the purges. The Soviet use of propaganda was prolific; it was just that under Stalin, graphic designers had no freedom to design as they wanted to.

Bibliography

Bayer, (1999) Art Deco Architecture, Thames and Hudson, London

Bourne J, Liddle P, & Whitehead I, (2001) The Great World War 1914 – 45 – 2 Who won? Who lost? - Harper Collins, London

Brendon P, the Dark Valley – A Panorama of the 1930s (2000) Jonathan Cape, London

Bullock A (1991) Hitler and Stalin – Parallel Lives, Harper Collins, London

Burns R (1995) German Cultural Studies an introduction, Oxford University Press, Oxford

Chickering R (1998) Imperial Germany and the Great War 1914 – 1918, Cambridge University Press, Cambridge

Colvin J, (2004) Decisive Battles, Headline, London

Crystal D, (1998) The Cambridge Biographical Encyclopedia, 2nd edition, Cambridge University Press, Cambridge

Faerna J M, (2000) Klee, Cameo/Abrams

Fulbrook, M (1991) the Fontana History of Germany 1918-1990 the Divided Nation Fontana Press, London

Ghirardo D, (1996) Architecture After Modernism, Thames and Hudson, London

Gropius W, The Imperative of Craft

Henig R (1998) The Weimar Republic 1919 – 1933, Routledge, London and New York

Hobsbawm E, (1987) The Age of Empire 1875-1914, Weidenfeld &

Nicholson, London

Hobsbawm, E (1994) Age of Extremes, the Short Twentieth Century 1914-1991, Michael Joseph, London

Holmes R, (1999) The Western Front, BBC Worldwide, London

James, H (2003) Europe Reborn – A History, 1914 – 2000, Pearson Longman, Harlow

Kenez P, (1992) Cinema & Soviet Society, Cambridge University Press, Cambridge

Kennedy P (1976) The Rise and fall of British Naval Mastery, Penguin, London

Pevsner N, (1995) The Sources of Modern Architecture And Design, Thames and Hudson, London

Rayner E, & Stapley R, (2006) History Debunked, Sutton Publishing, Stroud

Rees L, (1997) The Nazis – A warning from history, BBC Worldwide, London

Roberts J.M, (1996) A History of Europe, Penguin, London

Shirer W L, (1988) The Rise and Fall of the Third Reich, Arrow, London

Stevenson D, (2004) 1914 – 1918 A history of the First World War, Penguin, London

Watkins D (2005) A History of Western Architecture 4th edition, Lawrence King Publishing

Weimar Source Book

www.bauhaus/archiv